Written and Published By: Sunshine Creations
Illustrated By: Ali Pourazar
COPYRIGHT 2021 by Sunshine Creations. All rights reserved.

Today Ben took me outside to a place that he and his mother called the "yard".

There was a fence around the yard, but I squeezed through it and chased the neighbor's cat for a while.

While I was running in the yard, Ben went inside the house and came out with my blankie.

He started running while he was holding my blankie.

I wanted to show him how high I could jump. So, I chased him and jumped and snapped at my blankie a couple of times.

We were having so much fun but then Ben tripped over me and fell.

I was worried for a second, but then he started laughing and I knew he was fine.

I licked his face and then snatched my blankie and ran away.

Ben and I started playing tug. I was pulling on my blankie. I wanted to show him how strong I am.

I held on to my blankie with my teeth and pulled as hard as I could.

I pulled so hard that Ben had to let go.

He fell on his butt, and I ran around the yard with the blankie in my mouth. I was so proud.

Ben got up to chase me.
He was laughing and calling my name.

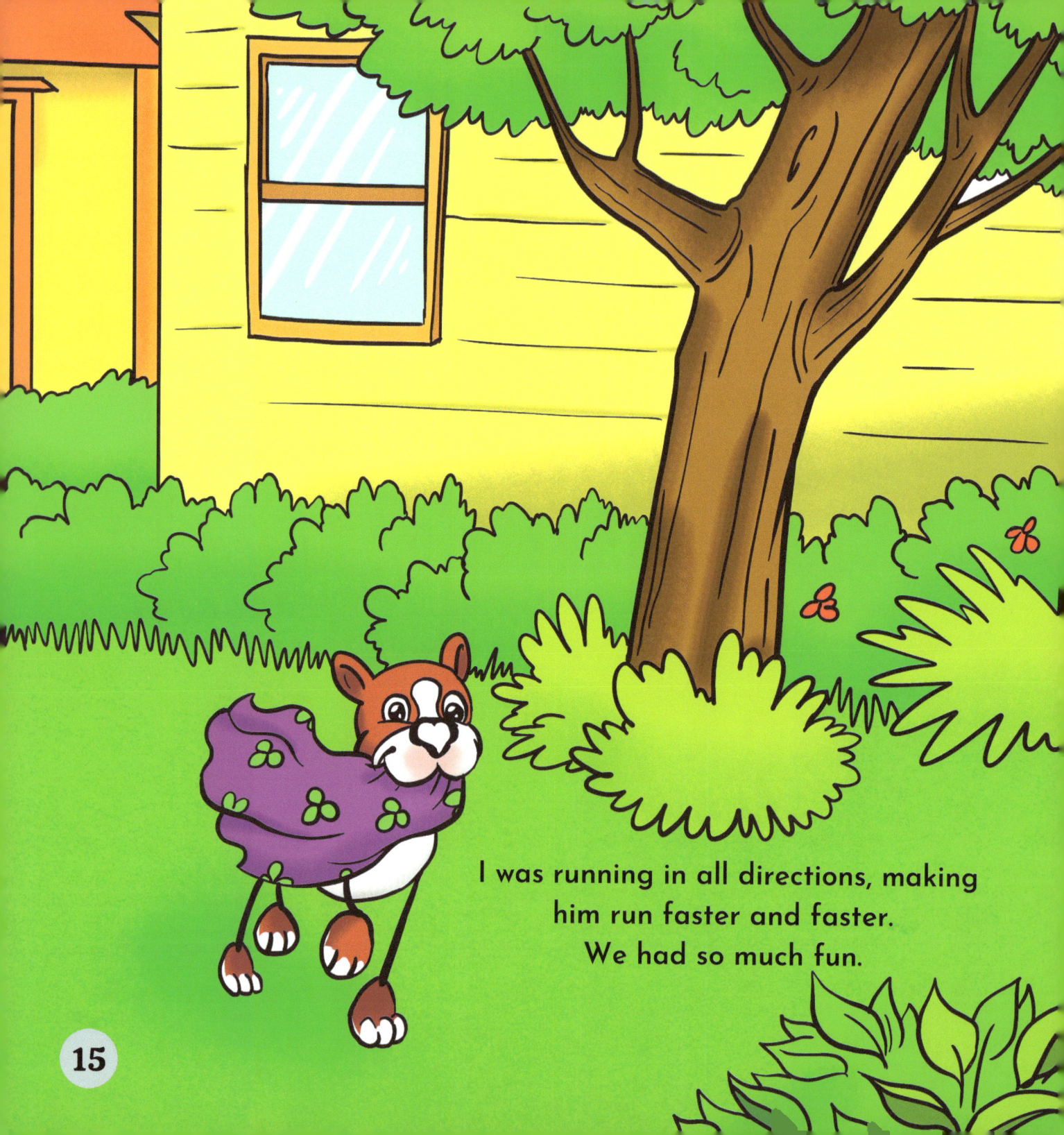

I was running in all directions, making him run faster and faster. We had so much fun.

Then we both got tired. Ben sat on the grass, and I sat beside him. We were both panting.

Ben laid on his back and I licked his face and his ears.

Then I realized my blankie was missing!

I could smell it, so I ran around the yard and looked everywhere but I couldn't find it.

"I think he's looking for his blankie. It's on top of the rose bushes." Said Ben's mom through the kitchen window.

Ben grabbed my blankie from the top of the rose bushes!

I love my blankie. It reminds me of my mommy and my and my brothers and sisters.

I loved playing in the backyard. I had an awesome time and can't wait to see what happens tomorrow.

Check us out in Instagram and Facebook:

 Facebook.com/sunshinecreations555

 Instegram.com/sunshinecreations555

Email us at: sunshinecreations555@Gmail.com

Check out Book #1, 2 & 3 in my Amazon author page

amazon.com/author/sunshinecreations555

www.ingramcontent.com/pod-product-compliance
Lightning Source LLC
Chambersburg PA
CBHW040023130526
44590CB00036B/68